W9-AWK-567

STUFF EVERY
WOMAN
SHOULD KNOW

STUFF EVERY WOMAN SHOULD KNOW

By Alanna Kalb

QUIRK BOOKS
PHILADELPHIA

Library of Congress Cataloging in Publication Number: 2018939433

ISBN: 978-1-68369-089-4

Printed in China

Typeset in Goudy and Transat

Interior design by Elissa Flanigan
Cover design by Andie Reid
Illustrations by Kate Francis
Production management by John J. McGurk

10 9 8 7 6 5 4 3 2

Quirk Books
215 Church Street
Philadelphia, PA 19106
quirkbooks.com

Stuff Every Lawyer Should Know: The publisher and author hereby disclaim any liability from an injury that may result from the use, proper or improper, of the information contained in this book. We do not guarantee that this information is safe, complete, or wholly accurate, nor should it be considered a substitute for a reader's good judgment and common sense. In other words: Exercise caution when parallel parking. Be safe when flirting with strangers. And never leave the house without safety pins.

To my mom,

who certainly doesn't need this book

but will buy twenty copies anyway

MIND, BODY, AND SPIRIT

THE
STUFF

Introduction

This book was not shortlisted for a Pulitzer Prize. It will not be read in classrooms, nor does it probe the condition of modern women pithily and with feeling.

But it does have good tips for how to talk to anyone anywhere. It'll help you write thank-you notes and master throwing a football. Is this book full of girly stuff? Yes. It will tell you how to stop a run in your stockings and advocates for batting your eyelashes if that gets you what you want. You'll learn to dress for your body type, what colors suit you best, and how to sew a hem.

But this book will also prepare you to ask for a raise, parallel park, and protect yourself with self-defense techniques. And of course every woman should have a handle on her oil pan. You don't want to gunk up the engine now, do you?

After many hours of research—sniffing my way through an upscale perfume boutique, asking a car salesman for bargaining tips—I realized one thing: no matter what you're doing or whom you're talking to, stand up straight, pull back those shoulders, and smile. It's called *confidence*.

Don't have any? Fake it. That is covered here too.

DO-IT-
YOURSELF

How to Change a Tire

This minor emergency is bound to befall you sooner or later, so be prepared. Know the necessary steps before it happens, and you'll save yourself a lot of stress.

1. As soon as you notice you have a flat, stop driving. Pull over onto a smooth concrete area with no slope and engage the emergency brake.

2. Most cars are equipped with a spare tire, jack, and lug wrench (the manual will tell you where to find them, but typically they're in the trunk). Carefully read the directions before using these items. Two things you won't find next to the lug wrench but will be glad you kept there: a blanket to put between your new jeans and a dirty highway, and some heavy gloves—grease is a lot harder to remove than nail polish.

3. While the tire is still on the ground, use your lug wrench to loosen the lugs (the bolts that keep your tires in place) just a little. That will make removing them easier once the car is jacked (raised off the ground). Think *righty tighty, lefty loosey*: attach the lug wrench in the direction you

want to turn it, parallel to the ground, and turn the wrench to loosen the lugs. You may need to use your foot to push down and loosen the lugs.

Turn the wrench to loosen the lugs.

4. Refer to the car's manual to determine the right spot at which to jack up your car. There is usually a little notch or lip in the side of the car where the jack should go. Jack up the car.

5. Completely unscrew the loosened lug nuts and remove the flat tire.

Be sure to jack up your car at the right spot.

6. Line up the spare with your lug bolts and push it in as far as you can. Because the tire won't simply rest flush on the bolts by itself, you'll need to hold it in place to properly screw on the nuts.

7. Now begin to replace the lug nuts. Screw them on with your hands as much as possible; then grab your lug wrench and tighten as much as you can. Always tighten nuts across from each other rather than going around in a circle, and never

pull up when tightening—go with gravity and push down.

8. Lower your jack stand and finish tightening your lug nuts using your foot (see step 3). You want them to be as tight as possible.

9. Spares aren't made to be driven on for long. Put your tools and flat tire in the trunk and drive to the closest gas station. If the tire isn't too damaged, the mechanic may be able to plug it; otherwise you'll need to replace it.

"Every time I go to a mechanic, they look at me like I'm stupid, 'It's a gasket, honey.' I know what a gasket is; it's $150. But a 'gasket, honey' is $200."

—Emily Levine, American comedian

How to Sew a Hem

Even if you don't know the first thing about sewing, you can learn to sew a basic hem, which will save you an unnecessary trip to the tailor.

1. Thread a sewing needle with approximately two feet of thread. Knot the two ends of the thread together near the bottom.

2. Turn the garment inside out, with the hem facing you.

3. Firmly attach the knotted end of the thread by making one or two stitches on the underside of the garment (so the thread won't show when you're wearing it).

4. Make a hem stitch by pushing the needle from the underside of the garment to the front, keeping in mind that the stitches should show as little as possible on the front of the garment. Repeat along the length of the hem.

5. If the material is heavy, just pick up some of the threads with the needle; don't go all the way through to the front. For thin fabrics, catching only one thread is necessary (really!). Don't

Hem stitch

pull your stitches too tight; a hem stitch should look like a loose zigzag.

Shortcut: Never underestimate the power of hem tape. You'd be amazed at how many things you can achieve with an iron (you do know how to iron, right? If not, see page 20) and some hem tape, no sewing necessary. Pants too long? Hem tape. Shortening curtains? Hem tape. Anything that needs to be stuck together in a straight line can be done quickly and easily with hem tape. And it's cheap, too.

Other Sewing Techniques

Here's how to quickly mend other minor sartorial emergencies that always pop up at inopportune moments.

- **Fixing a ripped seam:** Turn the garment inside out and lay it flat. Before starting to sew, you may want to hold the fabric in place with a few pins. Then sew the ripped section along the crease of the original seam using small backstitches: after your first stitch forward, backtrack half a stitch from where you started, go forward and backtrack again half the new stitch, then forward again. This will make the fabric react as if it were sewn on a machine, which is necessary because sewing in a straight line will make the fabric fall and stretch differently in that one section than in the rest of the seam.

Backstitch

- **Fixing those strange little frayed-at-the-edges holes in jackets and T-shirts:** Use thread that matches the clothing's color as closely as possible, opting for a shade slightly darker rather than lighter. Thread the needle and knot the ends. Sew from the back of the garment so that the knot and stitches are hidden. If you're working with knits or jersey, be sure to catch an intact stitch on all sides of the hole. Secure your handiwork with small backstitches and finish by bringing your needle once or twice through the loop created between thread and fabric.

- **Fixing loose lining in a coat or jacket:** Thread your needle and make a few small stitches in the fabric to secure it. Knot the end of the ripped thread to your new thread to prevent further unraveling. Sew inside the crease of the folded underlining using small stitches. When finished, knot your thread and the loose thread at the other end of the former rip.

How to Iron

If you plan to iron more than the occasional blouse, invest in a good-quality ironing board and an iron that has a steam setting and self-cleaning feature. Always remember: you can iron something nicely only if it's laid flat.

- Familiarize yourself with the iron's settings; fabrics need varying levels of heat. (Don't iron silk or a synthetic on the wool setting or you'll have a puckered, melted mess!)

- Fill the water reservoir if you plan to use steam.

- Read the care instructions on any garment you plan to iron. If there are none, try to determine the fabric and select that setting. When in doubt, always start on a cooler setting and test the temperature on a less obvious spot before ironing the entire garment.

- Acrylics may stick to a hot iron; velvets may become permanently shiny. To avoid mishaps, turn the garment inside out or place a clean cotton cloth, or press sheet, between the garment and the iron.

- Make sure no fabric is bunched up under the area you're ironing.

- For best results on cotton, iron when the fabric is still a bit damp. If it's completely dry, mist it with water, roll it up loosely, and let it sit for a minute before ironing.

- Move the iron slowly, being careful not to leave it in one place (unless you want an iron-shaped scorch mark there). Spray stubborn wrinkles with water and iron in a figure-eight motion.

- When ironing collared shirts, you'll have a much easier time if you use a sleeve board. Fold the sleeves in half vertically and iron down the middle from both sides, avoiding the fold so that you don't iron in a crease. Pull the sleeves over the sleeve board and iron. Then do the back, the sides, and the front, using the tip of the iron to reach between the buttons. Lay the collar flat and iron it on both sides. Avoid ironing it down, which will make it look flat. Fold the collar and bend it over your knee to give it a curved shape.

How to Check Your Oil

Oil is necessary for the proper function of your vehicle; it lubricates and reduces friction in the motor. Without enough oil, your engine can seize up, effectively ruining your car. You should change the oil as often as the car manufacturer recommends (usually between 5,000 and 7,500 miles). And make sure you're using the proper type for your car. Follow these steps to check and adjust the oil level.

1. For a proper reading, park the car on level ground and turn off the engine. Have a rag handy that you're okay staining with oil.

2. Pop the hood and locate the dipstick, which will be close to the front of the engine. (Consult the owner's manual if you can't locate it.) Pull it out and wipe it clean with the rag.

3. Reinsert the clean dipstick all the way. Remove it again, making sure to keep it pointing down. Do not turn it upside down, because any oil trickling upward will throw off the reading.

4. Hold the dipstick diagonally pointing down, and support the tip with your rag. Look for

*The oil level should be between the two
etched lines at the bottom of the dipstick.*

two lines etched at the bottom of the dipstick. Ideally your oil level will be between those lines. Depending on your vehicle, the low level may be marked with the word "low" or "add," instead of lines.

5. If your oil level is above the top line, you need some removed and probably need an oil change. Over-oiling causes oil to foam and can damage engine components.

6. If your oil level is below the bottom line, add a little. Unscrew the oil cap on the top of your engine (look for the oil symbol, which resembles a genie's lamp). Using a funnel, pour in half a quart of oil, taking care not to overfill. Start the car, and go for a short drive. Then check the oil again and see if you need more. If you do, add another ¼ quart.

How to Remove a Stain

Fresh stains are always easier to remove than old ones, so treat them as soon as possible. If you're away from home with no rescue at hand, a douse of club soda helps prepare the area until you can apply the proper remedy. Remember these few general tips.

1. Use cool water when first rinsing a stain; warm water might set it in the fibers of the fabric.

2. Scrape off or blot whatever caused the stain, as much as possible. Then sponge with cold water or apply a pretreatment, working from the center of the stain outward.

3. Never iron a stain or throw it into the washing machine without pretreating.

Different stains call for different treatments. Here are some of the most common.

• **Red wine:** Blot with a paper towel and then pour salt onto the stain. If that doesn't remove it completely, combine one cup hydrogen peroxide with one teaspoon laundry detergent, pretreatment, or dish soap. Soak a clean sponge in the mix, squeeze out the excess, and blot the stain until it's gone. Then wash the garment according to the laundry instructions.

- **Lipstick:** Sponge with cool water and then apply liquid detergent or pretreatment directly to the stain.

- **Grease (mayonnaise, machine oil, etc.):** Use a pretreatment as soon as you can, and wash soon after applying. If you can't wash the fabric (if the stain is on a couch, for example), sponge on a stain-removal product. Apply an absorbent such as cornstarch or cornmeal if you're worried about the product staining the fabric.

- **Blood, chocolate:** Rinse in cool water and then apply a pretreatment. Wash in cold water with detergent.

- **Wax:** Harden the wax with ice or put the garment in the freezer. Once the wax is frozen, scrape off as much as possible; then wash with detergent in the hottest water the fabric can handle. Repeat if needed, and don't dry until the wax is completely gone.

- **Ink:** Apply a pretreatment and then wash with detergent in the hottest water the fabric can take. Or spray on a little hairspray until the stain disappears.

- **Grass:** Apply a pretreatment or a detergent with bleach (very effective on grass stains). Pour some detergent on the stain and scrub vigorously. Let sit for 15 minutes and then wash in warm water. If the stain is still there, repeat this process.

- **Other stains, or when in doubt:** Rinse with cool water, apply a pretreatment, and wash with detergent following the instructions on the garment.

How to Parallel Park

This is an extremely useful skill, especially if you live in or frequently travel to a city, where you will inevitably need to maneuver your vehicle into a curbside space (or pay outrageous garage fees).

1. Pull up next to the car in front of the parking spot and line up your rear seats with theirs. Your passenger side mirror should be about two feet away from their driver's side mirror.

2. Begin to reverse, but don't turn your wheel yet. As a general rule you want to start turning the wheel in the direction of the parking spot once your car's rear windshield is even with the end of the other car.

3. As you're turning the wheel, your car will start to ease into the spot. Using the car behind you as a guide and looking in your rearview mirror, begin to turn your wheel in the opposite direction once you see your rear window meet the other car's passenger-side front windshield.

4. Start turning the wheel in the opposite direction. As you counter-steer you'll feel your car

Begin to reverse, but don't turn your wheel yet.

begin to straighten out, becoming parallel with the curb.

5. Once your car is close to the front bumper of the car behind you, drive forward again. Turn your steering wheel toward the curb to get closer to it. Then counter-steer again to keep your car straight (you don't want your tail in the road).

6. If your car still isn't close enough to the curb, pull forward in the spot as far as you can. Turn the wheel completely in the direction of the curb and then put your car in reverse, in that order. This will let you get closer to the curb, even with little space between your vehicle and the cars in front of and behind you. When you're getting close to the curb, counter-steer to get parallel with it. Pull your car forward. Repeat this process until your car is straight and parallel.

How to Fix a Fashion Emergency

From static cling to sticky cat hair, fashion emergencies take many forms and can cause much consternation. These tips will keep you looking perfectly polished.

- Hairspray lightly spritzed on your legs will keep silk skirts and other lightweight fabrics from clinging. You can also rub your legs with a dryer sheet.

- Carry an extra pair of stockings if you're going somewhere important in case you get a run. If you catch a run early, applying clear nail polish to the material will stop it in its tracks.

- For a broken heel or snagged fingernail, crazy glue is the answer (but use it sparingly). The bottle is small enough to pop in your purse.

- Stuck zipper? Rub a bar of soap or a wax candle over the sticky spot.

- For treating stains when you're out and about, nothing beats a stain-remover stick. If you don't have one, look for someone with an infant—baby wipes work in a pinch.

- Have a lint roller handy. You'll look more put-together without lint—or fur—stuck all over you.

- Safety pins hold up hems, fix broken straps, and rein in cleavage when the top button of your blouse pops off. Stash several in your purse for quick fixes.

- If your earring back goes missing while you're at the office, hold the bauble in place with a mechanical-pencil eraser. Trim it to size using scissors and then slide into place.

BUSINESS
AND
PLEASURE

How to Ask for a Raise

You've put in your time and worked your butt off, and now you deserve a raise. Good for you! So, what's the best way to get one? Read on.

1. First of all, try to be objective and realistic when determining whether you've earned a raise. Don't go by what your friends tell you. And whatever you do, don't say you *need* a raise. That implies you're asking for one because you can't pay your bills, not because your work merits more compensation.

2. When you start a job, it's a good idea to ask how salary increases are handled. If you didn't, check your company's policy on raises. If there's a formal policy or review, wait until you've reached the benchmark before starting the conversation.

3. Itemize your responsibilities as you understand them or as they were presented to you. Describe how you have performed your tasks and define your accomplishments. If your company conducts formal evaluations, refer to those as a guideline—but don't cite them verbatim. If

there is no formal review policy, try to remember positive comments your managers have made about your work. Again, use them as a guideline, but don't quote them exactly.

4. Set up a meeting with your manager for the sole purpose of discussing your pay level. Give sufficient notice; don't just wander in. Try to do so when you know your manager is in a positive mood.

5. Practice, practice, practice. Rehearse as you would for any presentation. Try to treat it as though you're arguing the case for someone else instead of yourself—it's best to stay unemotional when the topic is money.

6. At the meeting, make your case as you rehearsed it. Don't be intimidated by your manager's reaction or comportment. You're prepared for this, remember? Be upbeat and positive, not nervous or defensive.

7. Don't bring up what your friends earn for similar jobs. The last thing you want to hear is, "Then go work for that company." (However, you may want to research salary trends for your

industry and region, to have an idea of what someone doing your job makes at other similar companies. This will put your request in context and help you gauge an appropriate increase to ask for.)

NOTE: Common sense dictates that if your company is struggling financially, it's best to hold off on your salary-hike request. However, do make sure that management is aware that's why you're waiting. Tell your boss that you believe you've earned a raise but will wait until things look brighter. You'll appear as both a team player and a savvy employee aware of her worth. Well played.

How to Budget

You can't develop better spending habits unless you know where your money is going. Establishing a budget is the first and most important step toward saving money.

- Start by writing down everything you spend for one month, including coffee, magazines, gas, lunch, those shoes you had to have, and that cookie you bought on your way home from work. You'll be shocked by how much money you went through without noticing.

- Make a list of all your set monthly expenses that must be paid: rent/mortgage, car payments, utilities, insurance, credit card payments, groceries, student loan payments, etc. Then add all your extra but fluctuating expenses, such as movies and going out, dry cleaning, manicures, *everything*. Don't forget expenses that come up only a few times a year (such as memberships).

- Next, write down your income, allowing for taxes if they aren't automatically deducted from your pay. Figure out the difference between your income and your expenses. If you come up with a positive amount, that's the amount you're allowed to spend in that month. Once it's gone, it's gone. No using debit or credit cards. It's often easier to see where your money is going if you take it out in cash at the start of the month. You'll be less likely to spend it if you know there's nothing left when it's gone.

- If you're spending more than you're making, don't panic. Take a deep breath and think about what you can do without. Start with the list of extras—that's where you're going to have to cut back. Don't see it as denying yourself the things you enjoy. Imagine truly not being able to buy food or make mortgage payments. When you have maxed-out credit cards and no savings, these are real possibilities. What's better: shopping, or knowing you have enough money to pay your bills?

- Make note of little treats you can live without, or brainstorm affordable alternatives. Start making coffee at home every morning to replace your daily fancy latte, or do your own manicures. Your savings will add up quickly.

- Credit card companies make money because people buy things they can't afford. As long as credit card bills are a major chunk of your expenses every month, you're one of those people. Make paying off your high-interest-rate cards a top priority.

- Do whatever you must to rein yourself in and stop spending. If you blow half your paycheck the day you get it, have that half deposited directly into your savings account so you never even see the money. Take your credit cards out of your wallet so you're not tempted to use them. Pay with cash so you can see where your money goes. These measures may sound extreme (and impossible), but the reality is that, as enjoyable as the fun stuff is, it's absolutely useless when you need something to fall back on.

> *"Money isn't everything—but it ranks right up there with oxygen."*
>
> —Rita Davenport, humorist and writer

How to Ask for What You Want (and Get It)

You can't get what you want if you don't know what it is. Have an objective in mind before you open your mouth.

1. Whatever you're asking for, you'll get further by being pleasant. It's harder to scare someone into doing something than it is to charm them.

2. The "don't you know who I am" routine is annoying and embarrassing for everyone involved. However, you should be confident while also being friendly. Being convinced that you will get what you want while you're asking for it is the verbal equivalent of walking into a room with your shoulders back and your head held high.

3. What does the squeaky wheel get? The grease, of course. Ever been on the phone with your credit card company or landlord? Be calm, persistent, and *keep pushing* until the problem you want addressed is taken care of. If the person you're speaking with can't help you, ask for a supervisor. Smile, be nice, but don't budge

an inch until the person accommodates your request.

> **NOTE:** "Corporate" can also be a magic word when dealing with huge, inefficient companies. For example: "It's unfortunate you won't be able to help me. I guess I'll have to contact Corporate. May I have your name, please?"

4. Sticking to your guns is worth it only if your request is feasible. When someone clearly would do anything to get rid of you but isn't giving you what you want, it's probably because they can't.

How to Slow Dance

Back in the day, men and women were taught how to dance together—really *together*—as in waltzes and jitterbugs and foxtrots and other styles you need a partner for. These days you may require a quick written primer on dancing with someone other than your friends, in a circle, in a bar.

1. Wrap your arms around the back of your partner's neck; alternatively, you may place your left hand on his right shoulder and your right hand in his left hand. If your arms are around his neck, his hands should be either on your hips or clasped at the small of your back.

2. Sway back and forth gently and slowly, matching your movements to the music. You can stay in one place or move in a circle to keep things interesting. Either way, you don't need to move too much. Slide your feet back and forth, or transfer your weight back and forth from one foot to the other. Take care not to step on your partner's feet.

3. Let him lead. Yes, this goes against everything you believe in as an independent, self-assured woman. Do it anyway.

4. Make eye contact. You're not in middle school anymore, so acknowledging your dance partner instead of staring over his shoulder at your friends is both acceptable and encouraged.

Classic Slow-Dance Songs

The next time you're at a wedding and the DJ starts one of these down-tempo romantic numbers, you'll be ready.

- "At Last" by Etta James
- "Can't Help Falling in Love" by Elvis Presley
- "Crazy" by Patsy Cline
- "P.S. I Love You" by Billie Holiday
- "All of Me" by John Legend
- "The Lady in Red" by Chris de Burgh
- "Unforgettable" by Nat King Cole
- "Wonderful Tonight" by Eric Clapton

How to Throw a Football

The objective here is to impress your cousins on Thanksgiving or get the attention of that cute guy at the park, not to be drafted by the NFL. So relax and have fun.

1. Grip the ball about one-third of the way from the end with your dominant or throwing hand, cradling it in the U shape created by your thumb and fingers. Place your fingertips on the laces (those raised stitches).

2. Put your other hand on the ball and raise it to chin level. Step back with the leg on the same side as your throwing hand and bring your hand back, over you shoulder. Point at your target with your free hand (figure A).

3. Snap your arm forward, following through with your shoulders and hips. As you throw, shift your weight to your front foot (figure B).

4. Release the ball when your arm is slightly above your head and out to the side. Follow through with your arm.

How to Act Confident (Even When You're Not)

Here's the thing about faking confidence: do it for a while, and eventually you'll get so good at it that you might just *become* confident. Confidence will make you smarter, happier, and more attractive, guaranteed. That's because by appearing sure of yourself, you allow yourself (and others) to see how wonderful you are. And that's a good feeling. In fact, it only breeds more confidence.

- The basics are easy: stand up straight, with shoulders back and head up.

- When conversing with someone, don't whisper and look down. Make eye contact and speak clearly, as though you have something important to say, because you do.

- Firm up your handshake. Nothing makes a poorer first impression than a limp handshake, especially when accompanied by a mumbled "Hi" directed at the ground.

- Smile while speaking and take deep breaths to prevent squeaky-voice syndrome.

- Doing things slowly makes you look confident. This may sound silly, but quick, jerky movements look nervous and slapsticky. Even if you're quaking on the inside, "slow" translates to "calm and serene."

- The same goes for speaking in front of a group. Even if you've memorized every comma of your presentation, you will seem more confident and poised if you give the appearance of considering your words instead of blurting them out. Nothing says "I am uncomfortable doing this!" more than a speech delivered in fast-forward.

- You don't have to become a social butterfly, but making yourself interact with people will force you to become more comfortable with socializing. Don't be afraid of having nothing to say—truth is, you don't have to say anything at all. A conversation in which you do nothing but ask questions may seem inane, but your conversation partners will come away thinking you're the most interesting person they've ever met.

- The next time you feel awkward at a professional or social function, remember that many other people feel just as uncomfortable as you do. Adjust your posture, take deep breaths, and smile, smile, smile. You'll look more approachable, and you'll have something to focus on rather than thinking about how you want to sink into the floor.

• For many women, confidence comes with age and wisdom; speed up the process by becoming your own biggest fan. Instead of ripping yourself apart for everything that's wrong with you, recognize the things that make you fantastic, because there are a lot more of those. While you're working on that, keep your back straight, your head up, and flash those pearly whites!

> *"There's no better makeup than self-confidence."*
>
> —Shakira, Colombian pop singer and songwriter

How to Buy a Car without Getting Ripped Off

Let's be honest: If you walk into a car dealership whose employees are predominantly male, chances are the salesmen will be falling over themselves to help you. Here's how to make that attention work for you. This is some heavy insider information, so pay attention.

1. Do your research. If you have a specific car in mind, you should know what the car is selling for, if it has any documented problems, and if any rebates are available on it. Be aware of recalls and be wary of buying a new model that has just come on the market. You're better off waiting six months and then checking out feedback from consumers who have bought and driven that model. You don't want to place an order for a vehicle that you haven't even seen or driven. It could be littered with problems, but once you sign you're stuck with it.

2. Make a list of what you need versus what you want before you shop. You may need a car that

handles well in snow, but do you really need a sunroof? What are your buying "hot buttons": comfort, affordability, style, the sound system, drivability? Remember that the salesperson's job is to persuade you to spend more, whether or not you need NASA-approved seats or built-in Wi-Fi. You should go in knowing exactly what you care about, whether or not you have a specific car in mind.

3. You want to be taken seriously the minute you walk into the dealership. Be knowledgeable and clearly communicate what you want. Women have the edge of being . . . well, women, but this is not the time to pull the cute dumb-girl thing. Look professional and ask smart questions.

4. Shop around. Visit other dealerships to explore your options, but don't go overboard—every time a dealer performs a credit inquiry for car financing, your credit is affected. Pick three dealerships in your area so that you can take advantage of the services offered once you buy a car: free oil changes for the first year or free state inspections. You might be able to get a car for $500 less at one dealership, but if that same

car comes with great services elsewhere, paying more might be worth it in the long run.

5. The best time to go car shopping is at the end of the month, because both the salesperson and the dealership need to make their quota. And cars sitting on the lot cost the dealership money—they pay interest on them every month, so they're eager to unload them.

6. Know your credit score before you go, because dealerships may lie about your credit score in order to mark up your interest rate. If your interest rate is 9.9 percent at one dealership and 8.9 percent at another, you know the first dealership is holding something back. This gives you power; now you can tell them they need to beat a competitor's lower price if they want your business.

7. Consider joining a credit union for interest rates, since you'll get a much lower rate than you would from a dealership.

8. When at the dealership, don't just go into the showroom, test drive the car, and talk to a salesman. Walk around. Poke your head into

the service department to see what it looks like. Get a feel for the place; make sure they are nice and will offer excellent customer service. When you buy a car, you're also establishing a relationship with a dealership, and you want to make sure it's a long and happy one.

9. The dealership might not have the car that you want, but that doesn't mean they can't get it. Dealer trades are always possible, but they cost the dealership money, and most dealerships want to get rid of what they already have. Still, be aware that a dealership will go only so far to get you the car you want. And if you are incredibly picky, it is possible that the car you want doesn't truly exist.

10. Just because you're in a new environment and don't know the system doesn't mean that you have to give in and let yourself be steamrolled. You're the customer, so make the dealership work for your business. If the salesperson is using words you don't understand, tell him to stop and put it in layman's terms. Don't be shy, and don't let yourself be pushed into anything.

11. After you have all the paperwork in front of you, say that you'll take it home and think about it. Any respectable salesperson will let you do that, and a good one will ask, "What's it going to take for you to drive the car home tonight?" He's finding out what he needs to do to make the sale. Now he'll go back to his manager and try to make it work.

12. You found the perfect car. It has everything you need, the dealership offers great services, but you can't afford to pay the amount the salesman is insisting on. Ask this kick-ass question: "What's your holdback on that car?" In other words, you're asking what their markup is, or the difference between what the dealership bought the car for and what they're charging you. And if you really want to make them sweat, ask what the invoice is. The invoice is the price the dealership paid for the car, and as a consumer you shouldn't even know that dirty word. Consider that your last-resort question, because it's a powerful one. The dealership will always make a profit, even if they tell you you're getting the car at cost. And though you want the best deal you can possibly get, remember

that they're a business trying to make money, too.

Know Before You Go

Online comparison shopping is a great way to see how different vehicles, especially different makes, stack up against one another before you ever set foot on a showroom floor. Sites from car authorities like Kelley Blue Book and Edmunds, among others, let you compare multiple models at once and display everything from prices, dimensions, and interior and exterior features to warranty information, technical specs, and crash test ratings.

RELATIONSHIPS
AND
FRIENDSHIPS

How to Make Friends in the Real World

You never had to think about making friends in school. It sort of just happened, and you can't remember exactly how you did it. But now that you've entered the great big world, suddenly asking another woman to get lunch with you sounds, well, creepy. But learning to make new female friends is a crucial social skill—friendships are just as (if not more) important than relationships. So how do you go about nurturing friendships without coming across as a stalker?

- **At work.** This is likely where you spend the majority of your time, so what better place to look for friends? You already share something in common, and if you connect on another level with a coworker, start small. Invite her to grab a mid-morning coffee. Suggest a casual lunch if you're both stuck working through mealtime. Let friendships at the workplace develop naturally rather than coming off too strong.

- **Sports.** Gyms are highly social locations, especially if you take a group exercise class. Seeing the same women week after week provides the perfect opportunity for chitchat. Even better is joining an intramural adult league of a sport that you enjoy. You'll be getting exercise, plus team sports encourage social behavior. Most cities and towns have local running, hiking, or cycling clubs, or you can start one of your own on the internet. These will put you in contact with people who share a common interest, which is the first step in developing a connection.

- **Volunteer opportunities.** Helping others will allow you to foster connections with the people you're helping and with other volunteers. Many local organizations will match you up with an opportunity most suited to your time and interest level, helping groups dedicated to protecting or supporting children, the elderly, animals, low-income families, domestic-abuse survivors, the sick, or the environment.

- **Hobbies.** Whether your passion is knitting, art, music, wine tasting, gardening, comic-book collecting, poker, weight-loss support groups, young professional societies—whatever—there's a club

for it. Join! Enroll in a foreign language or a pot-
tery class. Sing in the choir at your church. Get
involved with local government. Just as with dat-
ing, you're never going to meet anyone if you stay
cooped up in your apartment with your cat. In this
day and age, there is a club for nearly everything.
Just look online to find what's available near you.

• **Online.** Nowadays, it's much more acceptable to
make initial connections online. Websites like
Craig's List have special categories for strictly
platonic encounters. People will post ads looking for a tennis partner or someone interested
in checking out a particularly obscure band.
There are even websites dedicated to connect-
ing women travelers and adventure seekers. Just
be sure to always be safe when meeting up with
strangers by informing a friend or family member of your plans.

• **Friends of friends.** If a family member or friend
(locally or in another city) knows someone who
lives near you, ask for an introduction (even
if it's just over email). You already have your
mutual acquaintance in common, so you're
more likely to hit it off. Also, there's a good

chance she has qualities that you look for in a friend since she's already friends with someone you care about.

- **Everyday locations.** Don't discount libraries, coffee shops, the grocery store, or the train. People tend to have routines, so it's likely you'll see the same faces frequently. This gives you the perfect opportunity to strike up a conversation. Chat up your neighbors. Talk to the girl you see every morning on your commute. Most people are generally friendly if you give them a chance.

Making friends might not be as easy or as natural as it was in school, but you just have to approach it in a different way. Make a point to put yourself in social environments where people are interacting. Sure, it might seem daunting at first to show up somewhere alone, but the more you put yourself out there, the more you'll feel comfortable in solo social situations. It's only a matter of time before you meet people with whom you connect.

How to Listen to a Friend

Listen is the key word, so remember to do exactly that. That means not telling her what to do, and definitely not interrupting with your own issues or a story to top hers.

1. Maybe she needs a little nudge to get talking. Asking "Is something on your mind?" will let her know that you've got time and a sympathetic ear.

2. You shouldn't be talking much, but occasional nods or *mm-hmms* are good to make sure she knows you really are listening. A blank stare and silence are likely to convey "I'm making a mental grocery list" more than "I'm paying attention to you."

3. If she asks for your opinion, try to put yourself in her position before offering advice. Even if you disagree with her perspective, never be condescending.

4. Remain objective. As a good friend, you won't always tell her what she wants to hear, but that's the point. Otherwise she might as well

be talking to a Magic 8-Ball. Just remember to watch your tone. If you're careful, you can tell her something she might not want to hear without coming across as insensitive or hypercritical.

5. If you've been through a similar experience and came out of it wiser/better/stronger, tell her about it and reassure her that she will too. Sometimes the best thing about talking out a problem is getting a reality check from someone who's been there, done that, and ended up just fine.

> "This is what we can all do to nourish and strengthen one another: Listen to one another very hard, ask hard questions, too, send one another away to work again, and laugh in all the right places."
>
> —Nancy Mairs, American writer

How to Flirt

Flirting is a playful way to express interest or gauge another person's interest in you. It can also be used innocently in situations that will not necessarily end up anywhere romantic. Whether you are a natural flirt or struggle with the concept, flirting is a fun and useful skill that any woman can master with a little practice. You'll undoubtedly find it to be quite handy at various times throughout your life.

- **Look approachable.** This is one of the first tips of successful flirting. If your arms are crossed and your shoulders are hunched over, you'll look as though you're avoiding interaction. Maintain an open stance, with good posture and shoulders back. Relax your muscles. Exude confidence without projecting arrogance.

- **Make eye contact.** A direct gaze is one of the most important tools in flirting. Studies have shown that, when talking, people look at each other only 60 percent of the time on average. Increased eye contact conveys interest without ever speaking a word. Although simple in concept, it's hard to master. Too little eye contact and the other person will think you're not interested; too much and you will look like an obsessed creepy stalker.

> **BONUS TIP:** To catch someone's eye from across the room, hold your gaze two seconds longer than you normally would. Look away and then glance back. If your eyes meet . . .

- **Smile.** A smiling face naturally draws people in and makes you feel more confident. Smiling projects the impression that you're having a good time, puts you in a good mood, and boosts self-esteem. So turn that frown upside down!

- **Engage him in conversation.** Your first chat doesn't need to be profoundly deep or well thought out. Start with small talk. Open with a comment about your surroundings, the music playing, a book he's holding, or a sporting event. Compliment him on his shirt, his watch, his shoes. "So, do you like kids?" is not flirtatious; it's off-putting. You want to open up *gradually*. Save your theories on why you think you have trouble committing for another time.

Casual and nonthreatening conversation starters will set the tone for a friendly exchange that isn't too provocative or forward.

- **Be yourself.** If he's talking about the comic convention he attended as a kid and you still have your old She-Hulk costume in the basement, tell him! Don't be afraid of appearing dorky, and don't even think about playing dumb. He'll figure out the truth sooner or later anyway.

- **Use humor.** You don't need an arsenal of jokes at the ready, but a witty comment here and there will lighten any mood, inject some fun into the situation, and make you more approachable. And unless they're really horrible, laugh at his jokes.

- **Use body language.** Touch his arm gently when talking. Move in closer. Casually touch your neck. Mimic, or mirror, his gestures and movements. Body language (whether conscious or subconscious) is an effective form of nonverbal flirting that is often more powerful than spoken language.

Remember to keep the interaction cheerful and friendly. Flirting doesn't always need to lead to the bedroom; sometimes it's just a light-hearted way to interact. Don't put so much pressure on yourself. He's probably just as nervous as you are, and when did having a conversation become such a big deal? If you get the feeling he's distracted or uninterested, throw out a cheery "It was nice talking to you" and be on your way. Next!

"There are few young women in existence who have not the power of fascinating, if they choose to exert it."

—Benjamin Disraeli, British prime minister and novelist

How to Give a Passionate, Mind-Blowing, Knock-His-Socks-Off Kiss

He won't know what hit him.

1. Lead into it with some yearning eye contact. Slip your arms around his neck and pull him close.

2. Start gently and take your time. An intense kiss requires build-up.

3. Don't try to swallow his lips. You are not a cow.

4. Go easy on the tongue. It's about quality, not quantity.

5. Like slow dancing, kissing needs a rhythm. Pay attention to the other pair of lips and stop trying to run the show.

6. Give your tongue a rest and try a little lip-nibbling and sucking (very effective, but best in moderation).

7. Finish it off with some soft pecks.

8. Pull away slowly with a dreamy gaze. Ahhh.

How to Deflect Unwanted Attention

As women, we tend to be quite aware of feelings: our own, our friends', those of that guy we met 60 seconds ago and don't want to offend. But some men won't pick up on a subtle refusal, so follow these steps to shut down an unwanted interaction, saving yourself 25 minutes and a series of increasingly tight smiles.

1. Be blunt. Say, "Thank you, I'm not interested." Don't bother justifying anything. As soon as he hears it's a no-go, his eyes will glaze over anyway.

2. But don't be bitchy. Unless he used a really horrible, sleazy pickup line (in which case, feel free to come back with one of the responses on pages 69–70), you can't blame the poor guy and his sweaty palms for trying. Smile and tell him, "No thanks."

3. If he's being pushy, don't get annoyed or angry. When he says, "Hey baby, can I take you out sometime?" smile and repeat yourself: "No thank you." If he's still hovering, tell it like it is: "I'm not interested." And if he still doesn't

get it, tell a bouncer or bartender that this person won't leave you alone.

4. If you know before going out that you won't be in the mood for any overtures all night, throw a ring on your left ring finger before walking out the door. That should keep away all but the creepiest of creeps.

NOTE: These tips should dissuade the occasional clueless barfly or acquaintance. If you're ever in a situation in which you feel threatened or unsafe, call the police. Don't forget to study the self-defense techniques on page 125—better to be prepared just in case.

Good Responses to Bad Pickup Lines

If your polite, respectful responses aren't being heeded, feel free to send a little snark his way.

"Hi. I'd like to call you. What's your number?"

"It's in the phone book."

"I know how to please a woman."

"Good, then please leave me alone."

"Haven't I seen you someplace before?"

"Yes, that's why I don't go there anymore."

"I would go to the ends of the earth to meet you."

"Yes, but would you stay there?"

"Your face must turn a few heads."

"And yours must turn a few stomachs."

"Your place or mine?"

"Both. You go to yours and I'll go to mine."

"How do you like your eggs in the morning?"

"Unfertilized."

"I can tell that you want me."

"Ohhhh. You're so right. I want you . . . to leave."

"Your body is like a temple."

"Sorry, there are no services today."

"Hey baby, do you have a minute?"

"Sorry, I'm fresh out."

"Is this seat empty?"

"Yes, and this one will be, too, if you sit down."

How to End a Relationship

The end of a relationship is never fun, whether you're on the delivering end or the receiving end. When you're the one ending the relationship, be mindful of the other person's feelings and try to make the experience as painless as possible.

1. You can't end a relationship before you're ready, but once you make that decision, commit to it. If the other person isn't ready for the relationship to end, he will likely try to talk you out of it, so you need to be strong and confident in your decision.

2. Often making a list of all the negatives can help solidify your decision. Write down negative feelings, arguments, or specific examples of times when you felt crappy in the relationship. This will help you drive home your point that you two are not the best match.

3. Deliver the news in person. No emails, phone calls, or text messages. As tempting as it may be to be passive-aggressive, this is the cowardly way to deal with things. Be an adult. You owe this person an honest explanation.

4. Calmly explain your points in a clear, honest, and straightforward manner. Be firm but polite. Don't ridicule or berate the other person. Plainly state your reasons why you are ending the relationship.

5. Do not lead the person on or give him false hope. If you think he is a good person, pay him a compliment and tell him why he's a great catch. Avoid placing blame. Instead refer to the fact that you two just aren't a good fit. You want to indicate that the breakup is due to a mismatch, not a personal flaw.

6. Breakups can be dramatic and emotional. Try to keep your wits about you. The calmer you are, the calmer the other person will be as well. Some people can become irrational, overly dramatic, or even violent. If you sense that will be the case, meet in a public setting, such as a coffee shop, or have a nearby friend or relative on call to be there at a moment's notice.

7. Avoid feeling guilty about the breakup or punishing yourself for your decision. Remind yourself of your reasons for choosing to end the

relationship, referring back to your list of negatives if necessary.

8. "Let's still be friends" never works. You need some time and space apart before a friendship is possible. Someday you may be able to have that kind of bond with this person, but immediately after the breakup you need to make a distinction and create emotional distance. Avoid physical intimacy with this person after the breakup—that will only complicate the matter and lead to more pain.

How to Cure a Broken Heart

You will despise the people who tell you you'll get over it. You'll want to scream that they don't know what they're talking about. But they do. And with time you will.

1. Wallow away. Initially you're likely to be in shock, which is the worst time to do anything other than let your feelings sink in. Go to the movies, watch TV, read a book (but limit yourself to lighthearted stuff *only*). If you must go the tearjerker route (there's nothing like more misery to accessorize your own, right?), have tissues on hand.

2. Talk a friend's ear off and/or write down your feelings. It's therapeutic, and a few months later you'll look back and be amazed at how upset you were over what's-his-name.

3. After a few days, your shock may be replaced by self-pity or anger. Either way you probably won't want to do too much yet, other than cry or punch things. For the latter, find a gym: you can develop great biceps while being mad and miserable, and a hard workout is a fantastic way

to improve your mood (or at least burn off some emotional energy).

4. Don't let yourself get fixed up with somebody new just yet, and don't go looking for anybody either. If you're alternating between crying miserably and laughing hysterically, you're not ready to look for a soul mate.

5. Cliché as that "get a hobby" stuff is, there must be something you've always wanted to learn, do, or see. Now is a good time to explore those interests and hobbies.

Initially, sympathy may be all that you can stomach. But when you're trying to move on, tough love is invaluable. Steer clear of friends who sympathize too much—that will only delay your progress. Once you come out of the dark mourning period, you'll have days when you find yourself hovering between relapsing and maybe feeling just a *little* bit better. Summon every ounce of self-discipline and force yourself toward the "feeling better" side. It will get easier every day. Eventually you won't need to force yourself to feel better because you really and truly will, and then you're on your way.

BEAUTY
AND
FASHION

How to Dress for Your Body Type

Clothes are supposed to complement your body, and proper fit is the most important factor when it comes to flattering your figure. The best way to dress for your body type is to know exactly what does and does not work on you.

- Take a good look at your body. What do you like about it? What would you rather hide? Some clothes make you look much better than others. Figure out what those pieces have in common and keep that in mind as you shop.

- Use common sense. When trying to minimize your bust, don't draw attention to it with ruffles or tight tops. To make a large derriere look smaller, wear dark-colored pants and skirts. For a tiny waist, wear shorter cardigans to emphasize it, not ones that hit at the hip.

- Look through your closet with a trusted friend who'll be honest about items that are worth keeping. If you've been telling yourself for the last three years that you'll wear that skirt again but you still haven't touched it, it's time to let it go. The only caveat: If it's a well-made, quality piece, store it (not in your closet) until you find someone who will love it as much as you did.

- It takes discipline to avoid clothes you love but that don't look good on you. So don't even go near them. You might relapse. Be strong. And always keep the receipt.

- It's not worth buying trendy clothes that don't suit you. Leggings may be everywhere, but if you're bottom-heavy or short, they shouldn't be on you.

- Be adventurous! Watch for new cuts and styles. Ask that brutally honest closet-helper to go shopping with you; she might suggest things you'd never pick up. Try everything, and if it doesn't make you look like a million bucks, leave it on the rack.

How to Have Style

Style reflects who you are, what you like, and what you feel good in. Plus, first impressions can last a long time. You don't have to be "into fashion" to have style, and having a unique look can create an instant effect.

- Clothes can make you feel like a new person, happier and more confident. Getting out of your everyday jeans and T-shirt ensemble and into something new for you is *not* a waste of time.

- Browse magazines and websites that feature clothes you like, and talk to friends whose style you admire. Once you know what you like (and why), you can pinpoint what works on your body. Getting dressed should be neither agonizing nor boring.

- Never wear something you can't carry off with conviction. If it doesn't feel good, it won't look good.

- Dress for yourself as much as for everyone else. It feels good to impress, but it feels even better to look in the mirror and think, *Wow, I look great!*

- Remember that clothes, shoes, hair, makeup, and jewelry all work together. Don't throw up your hands because investing in your appearance is all too much work; instead see it as an opportunity to look great and experiment.

- If you take risks with your makeup, hair, or clothes and you hate the result, don't freak out. None of these changes are permanent. It's better to try new things and take them off than never bother because you're afraid to look bad.

- Always have one or two no-fail outfits that you know look and feel terrific.

"Fashion changes, but style endures."

—Coco Chanel, French fashion designer

Ten Stylish Pieces Every Woman Should Own

When you find quality pieces you love and wear often, take care of them and they'll last for years. Also, consider shopping the way guys do—buy two of something you adore.

1. There is a reason for underwear (other than to be cute). A quality bra that fits correctly will make your breasts perkier, your back straighter, and your clothes fit better. The majority of women wear a bra that's the wrong size, so if you have a feeling you may be one of them, it's worth going to a department store or lingerie boutique for a fitting.

2. Cute little dress, great hair and makeup—why would you ruin it with a shapeless, boring coat? Your coat will be the first and sometimes the only thing people see most months of the year, so take the money you wanted to blow on a new handbag and get a good-looking, *warm* coat instead.

3. Jeans have become appropriate for nearly every occasion, so find a pair (or three) you love, feel

fabulous in, and can dress up or down. They'll last longer if you wash them inside out and keep them out of the dryer.

4. Get a basic black, wrinkle-free, jersey-blend wrap dress. It's good for work, nights out, fancy dinners, or afternoon coffee dates. It will create the illusion of a waist if you don't have one and emphasize it if you do. Pairing it with different shoes and accessories will let you wear this piece a dozen ways, and there is nothing easier to wash in the sink or throw in an overnight bag for a weekend trip.

5. Invest in a versatile blazer/jacket; try on different cuts and lengths to find the right one for your body type. Regardless of the style, it should fit well in the shoulders. Choose a color that will work with the rest of your wardrobe. It will dress up jeans and a T-shirt, go over dresses and tops, and help pull an outfit together.

6. Statement (i.e., bold and chunky) jewelry adds instant character to any outfit.

7. Scarves can do more than keep you warm. Get a few lightweight versions in several sizes (pocket square, large square, long and skinny, etc.) in colors that look great on you and you'll be wearing them all year-round.

8. Find pants (not jeans!) in a midweight, good quality fabric, at a length that will work with shoes you wear most often. A flattering cut is a must, so if you have to try on 35 pairs to find the best style, so be it.

9. Heels that can go from work to drinks—and stand a little walking in between—are a must-have. Look for versatile styles that you can wear with dresses, skirts, and trousers.

10. Find your perfect handbag. But note that *perfect* doesn't mean anything big enough to cram all of your stuff into; it means versatile and well-made with quality materials. Find a size and shape that complements your figure. Bags that hit at the waist will draw attention there. The same is true for hips.

What Colors Look Good on You

Wearing clothes in hues that suit you is one of the easiest ways to improve your appearance. A flattering cut won't do anything for you if the color makes you look washed out or sallow. Your best colors depend on your skin tone, as well as your hair and eye color. Here's how to identify them.

- Stand in front of a mirror in natural light. Find as many solid scarves and tops as you can and drape them over your neck and shoulders. Which colors make your eyes sparkle and your skin glow? Seek those out. Avoid colors that make you look unhealthy, yellow, or green.

- One way to determine your skin tone is to try on silver and gold jewelry: Silver usually looks better on cool tones, gold on warm tones. Neutral skin tones look good in both.

- Makeup should also match your skin tone and eyes. Some brands make foolproof palettes, a good way to experiment with different shades and combinations. Don't be afraid; it washes off.

- Be honest with yourself. If you love pastel pink but it doesn't work, kiss it goodbye. However, you don't necessarily have to sacrifice the color entirely. Try a shade of the same color—magenta or coral—with different undertones (say, bluish as opposed to reddish).

- If you've never worn a certain color, try it. You may be missing out on a hue that makes you look fantastic.

The chart on the next spread will help you determine what colors look best on you based on your skin tone.

SKIN TONE	
Cool	Blue or gray eyes. Blonde, brown, or black hair. Skin has blue and pinkish undertones, and the veins on the underside of your wrist look blue in natural light.
Warm	Brown, green, or hazel eyes. Brown, black, red, blonde, or strawberry blonde hair. Skin has yellow/orange or olive undertones, and the veins on the underside of your wrist look greenish in natural light.
Neutral	Eyes and hair can be any color. Skin undertones can be pink, olive, or yellow.

COMPLIMENTARY COLORS

Blues, silver, pure white, bluish red, pinks, purples, dark green. Most pastels. Jewel tones.

Terra-cotta, coral, red, burgundy, orange, gold, yellow, lighter greens, olive green, brown, off-white or cream. Earthy tones.

Most colors look good on you, but usually neutral skin tones will lean either toward cool or warm colors. Figure out which classification suits you better.

How to Age Gracefully

You're going to get older whether you like it or not. Youth may fade, but if you take care of yourself, your looks and zest for life don't have to.

- No matter how old you are, take care of your mind, body, and skin. Try to eat well and exercise, use moisturizer and sunscreen, and pay extra attention to sensitive areas, such as your eyes.

- Eat foods that make you feel good. Bodies change as they age, so don't expect to eat the same junk that you did when you were younger and could let your metabolism deal with it.

- Wear age-appropriate clothes that fit you properly. If you're having trouble shopping on your own, go to a reputable boutique for a consultation to discuss what types of clothing suit you and for which occasions. The money you'll spend on clothes the first time around will be worth it for the advice.

- Your skin and face change as you age, and that glittery eyeliner you wore at 25 just doesn't work anymore. If you're unsure about which direction to go, an aesthetician will help you find makeup and application methods that will work for your face.

- Accept your maturity, but try to mix with people of all ages. You'll have a better, more interesting perspective on life.

- Never stop cultivating friendships and doing things you enjoy. Learn new things, and travel when you can. Your brain won't age if you keep it in shape.

- If getting older is making you miserable, there's nothing to do but figure out why and try to get past it. Maybe you're outgrowing your old routine and it's time for a change: a relationship overhaul, healthier living, even a different job. Don't be surprised if the stuff you thought was fun in your youth isn't cutting it anymore—adapt your life to fit the wiser, more mature person you're becoming.

Purse Essentials

A woman's purse is her lifeline. Okay, so men may make fun of us ("What is *in* there?!"), but sure enough something in your purse has come to his rescue at some point. What would we do without it? Wallet, cell phone, and keys aside, here are some things you don't want to be without.

- Tissues: For spills, a messy sneeze, makeup application/touch-up, etc.

- Makeup: No need to drag around a full-size cosmetics bag. Toss in essentials *only*—lipstick or gloss, concealer, and a powder compact with a mirror.

- All-purpose cream or lotion

- A mini Swiss army knife

- Bandages

- Aspirin

- A stain-remover stick

- Pepper spray

A woman's purse is her lifeline.

- Matches or a lighter

- A needle and thread for fashion emergencies

- Hand sanitizer

- Breath mints

- A little notepad and pen

- Nail file

Occasionally go through your purse and remove the stuff you no longer need (your back will thank you). Consider your lifestyle. What do you need and use often? Get pocket-size versions of the must-haves. Be prepared, but travel light.

How to Pick a Signature Scent

One of the most enduring ways to leave an impression is with a stunning fragrance that follows you wherever you go. So take time to choose a scent that is unique to you—not what everyone is wearing at the moment. Investing in a good-quality perfume is a guilty—but a lasting—pleasure.

1. Have something in mind before you start shopping for a fragrance. Think in broad terms of smells you like: florals, fresh citrus, spicy, woodsy, etc. You may wind up getting something totally different from what you thought you wanted, but at least you'll have a starting point.

2. Scent is incredibly individual, and perfumes can smell entirely different on your skin than on a strip of paper. If you're thinking of buying something, spritz yourself, walk around a little, and come back if you really like it.

3. Since your body puts its own stamp on a scent, there's a good chance that a men's cologne will smell fantastic on you (and much more interesting than that girly flowery-vanilla standard).

Don't be afraid to wander over to the men's counters and ask for samples.

4. After a few spray-and-sniff cycles your nose will be tired; give it a break by smelling your scarf or sleeve. Some perfume connoisseurs insist coffee beans are the trick, although the only thing they do is take your nose in a completely different scent direction.

5. If you find a scent you love, there's nothing wrong with wearing it for years. Don't buy into the summer/winter rule, either. While citrusy perfumes may seem more appropriate for summer just by virtue of being light, that doesn't mean you can't wear a single perfume year-round.

6. Here's a tip from a long-time parfumeur: If you're fragrance-shopping in a large department store, don't expect a lot of help. Most salespeople won't know much about their merch, and the first note that will hit you in every scent is alcohol. With the exception of a few (such as Chanel No. 5), most mass-market perfumes are made with cheap or synthetic

ingredients. If you're looking for something unique, with depth and layers of scent, go to a boutique fragrance store. Even if you don't buy anything (be prepared, quality perfume isn't cheap), you'll leave with enough samples to last a while and an appreciation for the art of scent.

Preserving Perfume

Once you've settled on a signature scent, get the most out of your purchase by storing perfume in a cool environment away from light and fluctuations in humidity. That means don't keep it in your bathroom, which fills with steam every time you bathe. Instead, try a dark, cool closet or even the refrigerator; if the bottle was sold in a box, store in this original packaging. And keep the lid on the bottle between uses to prevent oxidization from weakening or altering the fragrance.

Essential Makeup Tips

If your hair and makeup are perfect, you can wear a T-shirt and jeans and look like a million bucks. The following tips will help you put your best face forward.

- The point of makeup is to make you feel and look good, not to be a chore. You needn't spend an hour a day applying it (unless you want to); five minutes is enough for light, natural-looking makeup that enhances your features.

- If you want to wear makeup but have no idea where to start, a consultation will familiarize you with what makeup can do and how to apply it. Contact your local beauty salon or spa for an appointment.

- No amount of makeup can cover unhealthy skin. There are a ton of skincare lines in different price ranges, so there's no excuse not to take care of your complexion.

- Makeup looks different according to changes in light and temperature. You may prefer cream blush to powder in the winter, for example, because it's heavier and combats pasty winter skin. Change your routine and products with the seasons and as you get older.

- Try to apply your daytime makeup in natural light. Artificial lighting can cast odd shadows and make colors appear different or lighter than they actually are. But if you'll be under fluorescent lighting all day, apply makeup in the same or similar light.

- A good concealer (for under-eye circles and blemishes) and powder (to set makeup and reduce shine) are necessary. However, unless you think you really need it, avoid foundation; it will look cakey if not blended properly, and your skin will be healthier if you let it breathe. Try tinted moisturizer instead.

- Blush gives your face definition. Choose a shade that won't look painted on; rather, it should look like you've been out for a brisk walk.

- Mascara is vital and will wake up your entire face. There are hundreds of options out there: lengthening, strengthening, volumizing, curling, all of the above. Find one that doesn't clump or flake.

- Many women swear by eyelash curlers. Try one to give your eyes that wide-open look.

- For a healthy glow, dust a light bronzer on your brow bone, temples, and to the left and right of your chin along the jaw line. Skip this step if you're wearing a high collar; your shirt will end up more bronzed than you.

- Lid primer will help eyeshadow last longer and increase the color's intensity.

- You hear it a lot because it's true: If you apply dark, dramatic eye makeup, go easy on the lips. And vice versa.

- Bright lipsticks, like red, require maintenance. Apply, blot with a tissue, dust with powder, put on another coat, blot, more powder, and a final coat. You'll still need to reapply, but the underlayer will help prevent that '90s lip liner look. A more straightforward solution is to wear long-lasting lipstick, but be aware that this stuff really does last.

- You should enjoy your makeup, but it also needs to be appropriate for your lifestyle. If you work at a straitlaced office, save the false eyelashes for the weekends.

- Well-groomed eyebrows make a huge difference in your appearance. How thick or thin they should be depends on the shape of your face. Turn to page 100 for tips.

Oval: Small eyebrows with a moderate arch are best. Keep them thick in the middle and trim at the ends. The beginning and end of the eyebrow should be on the same level, and the whole eyebrow should be about the length of the eyes.

Round: Long eyebrows with a high arch and thin ends that angle downward look best with this face shape. The eyebrow should end a bit higher than it starts.

Square: Stick to small, crescent-shaped eyebrows that slide from both sides. Keep them thick and bent in the middle.

Triangular: Thick and straight eyebrows are best for triangular faces. One-third of the outside end should bend down. Eyebrows should be thicker to de-emphasize the jaw line; steer clear of thin eyebrows. The eyebrow should begin and end on the same level.

Pear-Shaped: Create straight eyebrows that aren't very long, but have pointed ends.

A professional should know what will look good, but feel free to describe what you like and see if it works for you.

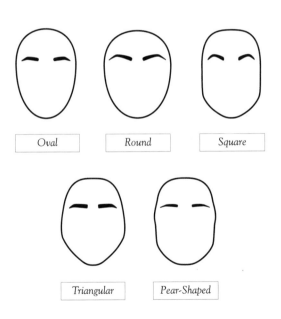

Oval

Round

Square

Triangular

Pear-Shaped

ETIQUETTE
AND
SOCIALIZING

How to Give and Accept a Compliment

"I love your shirt!"

"Oh, it's so wrinkled . . . I found it in the bottom of my closet, I never wear it because it makes me look fat but I have no clean clothes and . . ."

Stop. None of this demoralizing drivel. Here's how to acknowledge a compliment and pay it forward.

1. When someone compliments you, smile and say "thank you." Throw in a witty (not self-derogatory!) response, if you're so inclined. But please, don't use the opportunity to deflect the praise or put yourself down.

2. If the girl who sits a few cubicles down from you is wearing a color that suits her, tell her so. Hearing your comment will make her day, and you'll feel good about making someone else feel good. It's win-win. But . . .

3. Only give a compliment if you mean it. An insincere compliment is far worse than no compliment at all. You'll appear fake, and the other person will wonder why you're being a jerk.

Even worse is overly complimenting someone in an attempt to suck up or make nice. People see right through it.

4. Few people don't like hearing and talking about themselves. If you're introduced to a new person and the tone is chilly, flash a bright smile and find something to compliment. Odds are the interaction will warm up a little and the ensuing conversation will be that much more pleasant.

How to Write a Thank-You Note

Your mother was right. At some point, you will encounter a situation that calls for a thank-you note. Not a thank-you phone call. Not a thank-you email. A good old-fashioned handwritten thank-you note mailed to the gift giver. Whether it's for a book, electric juicer, bouquet of flowers, or tin of homemade cookies, thank-you notes are a thoughtful and personal way to express gratitude for a gift kindly given and happily received.

Before You Start

- Buy paper you like. Pretty stationery, a greeting card, or a neutral notecard will do the trick.

- If you're nervous about writing the note, do a draft first.

- Most important: Send it quickly. A thank-you note received two months after the gift loses its charm.

1. Address the person by name. Depending on the relationship, you can use "Dear," "Hi," or begin with the person's first name. "Dear" is always a safe bet.

2. Say "thank you." And please, without the *I am just writing to* or *I just wanted to say* . . . Both are unnecessary. *Thank you so much for* . . . will do nicely. Also, steer clear of mentioning specific amounts of money. Words like *generosity* sound much better than *fifty dollars*, as in, "Thank you for your generosity."

3. Mention how you will use the gift. One or two sentences suffice: "I have been cooking a lot lately, and the blender will come in handy."

4. Refer to the past, allude to the future. Some variation of *It was wonderful* . . . and *I look forward to* . . . , with the specifics filled in, takes care of this step: "It was wonderful running into you at Lauren's Christmas party, and I look forward to seeing you at the annual barbecue." If the person is someone you barely know, never see, and don't expect to run into anytime soon, go with the failsafe "I am thinking of you and I hope all is well."

5. When writing a thank-you note, closing with a second thank-you isn't overdoing it—that's the point, after all.

6. *Sincerely, Love, Best regards* . . . pick an appropriate sign-off and sign your name underneath.

Thank-you notes need not be lengthy. A short, gracious, and genuine message will fulfill proper etiquette requirements.

Classic Go-To Drinks

Chances are someday you'll find yourself in a bar or restaurant where you are completely out of your element and baffled by what to order. Maybe you're a jeans-and-T-shirt kind of girl who finds herself at a fancy restaurant where the drink list is in another language, or you swear by pinot grigio and find yourself in a local bar where they only serve shots and beer. Perhaps you are at a work dinner with clients and want to order something a little more classic and less frou-frou than an appletini, or are on a first date and want to choose something classic and safe.

Either way, it's crucial to know what to order in a pinch. No need to break a sweat, just consult the chart on the next page for the classic go-to drinks to order in any situation, and no one will have any idea that you're about as comfortable as a fish out of water.

> *"Three be the things I shall never attain: envy, content, and sufficient Champagne."*
>
> —Dorothy Parker, American writer and critic

DRINK: Cosmopolitan

WHEN/WHERE TO ORDER:
Checking out a trendy new
lounge or club with your
girlfriends

DRINK: Vodka Tonic

WHEN/WHERE TO ORDER:
Dining with your boss and/or
clients at a steakhouse

DRINK: White Wine
(pinot grigio, chardonnay,
sauvignon blanc)

WHEN/WHERE TO ORDER:
At a wedding/late afternoon
lunch/dinner at a high-end
restaurant

DRINK: Light Beer

WHEN/WHERE TO ORDER:
Shooting pool at the local dive
bar with your boyfriend and
his buddies

DRINK: Bloody Mary

WHEN/WHERE TO ORDER:
Brunch

DRINK: Red Wine
(pinot noir, merlot, shiraz,
cabernet sauvignon)

WHEN/WHERE TO ORDER:
On a first date

How to Host a Cocktail Party

You don't need to serve an eight-course feast, make dessert from scratch, or decorate your home à la Martha Stewart to throw a fun and memorable cocktail party. What it really comes down to is making your guests feel welcome and comfortable. It's all in the planning.

1. Create a schedule of when to do what. There are several online resources to help you navigate a party timeline. Cutting up veggies the night before will free up precious minutes to concentrate on more pressing details the day of the party.

2. Stick to finger foods. Appetizers such as pigs in a blanket, mini quiches, veggies and dip, nuts, fruit, shrimp and cocktail sauce, deviled eggs, or tea sandwiches are easy options that will fill up your guests while allowing them to eat and chat standing up. Save the four-course meal for when you're trying to impress the in-laws.

3. Be prepared for early arrivals, and don't make getting dressed the last thing you do. Better to be chatting in the kitchen while whipping up

a dip than greeting guests in your bathrobe and bunny slippers.

4. Whether people are coming over for an evening or spending a few days at your home, you want them to feel at ease. Open the door with a smile, welcome them in, take their coats, and show them to the living room or spare bedroom. These gestures may seem old-fashioned, but they'll be appreciated because they make your guests feel at home.

5. People notice and appreciate little touches: fresh flowers on the table for a dinner party, towels and a pair of slippers by the bed for overnight guests. Think about what made you feel good the last time you were at someone's house and copy it. That said, don't fret about the dust on the baseboards in the playroom. Trust me, your guests won't notice. (And even if they do—so what?)

6. Of course you want to make sure everyone is happy, but don't forget to relax enough to have fun! Just remember that people are relying on you for drinks, food, and directions to

the bathroom, so keep your wits about you (in other words, lay off the booze).

7. Rope someone into being your right-hand woman. If you get overwhelmed, you can delegate responsibilities, pull her into the kitchen to help you, or just make her responsible for keeping Tipsy Tom and the tequila away from each other.

8. Don't sweat the small stuff. People traipsing through your house can be nerve-wracking, but don't worry about being a "perfect" hostess. Stay calm in the face of minor disasters. Spilled wine is not the end of the world (nor is it permanent; see page 25), and it will inevitably make for a good story the next time you all get together and laugh about your friend's klutziness.

9. Remember that it doesn't take a lot to impress. People are just happy to have a pleasant place to socialize. Some pretzels in a bowl and a good atmosphere often turn out to be the best time you and your friends have had in ages.

How to Talk to Anyone, Anywhere

The art of small talk is one worth cultivating. Here are a few tips for navigating a cocktail hour or a slightly awkward office-holiday party.

1. Smile. It will let people know you are receptive and friendly. You'll feel more comfortable striking up conversations with strangers if you stand up straight and act confident. (If you need to fake it, see page 46.)

2. Start with something neutral that requires more than a one-word answer. If you're nervous, keep it simple: "So, how do you know Justin?" or "What's a good place to eat around here?" If you can't come up with an opener, pay the person a (sincere) compliment.

3. Ask lots of questions. Everyone likes talking about themselves.

4. If you've tried every trick in the book and Susie's still icy, maybe she's just having a bad day. Say you need to go grab another drink and move on to a friendlier stranger.

5. Sometimes friendliness can backfire, like when the IT guy warms up to you at the office party and starts giving you a detailed description of his action-figure collection. In that case, tell him you have to go get some water, or make sure your cube mate is going easy on the wine, and bow out gracefully. If you feel bad, rope someone else into the conversation and, after a minute, use your line and leave them to it.

Conversation Topics to Avoid with Strangers

1. Health issues

2. Long recaps of books or movies

3. Offensive or off-color jokes

4. Anything personal or embarrassing about you, your friend, or your significant other

5. Politics or religion

6. Money

How to Tip

A friendly "thank you" is good, but a tip is better. The only time you shouldn't tip is if the person providing the service is the owner of the establishment. When abroad, make sure to read up on the local customs. Tipping varies by country.

- **Restaurants:** Unless the service was so horrible that you simply can't stomach the idea of giving money to your server (although many people will typically leave 10 percent in this situation), the general rule of thumb is 15 to 20 percent of the bill. Many establishments automatically add a gratuity to the bill for groups of six or more, in which case you don't need to add a tip.

- **Taxis:** Add a few dollars to the total. If the driver got you there fast or helped you load eight suitcases, add another buck or two.

- **Valet parking** generally calls for about five dollars, but remember that wages for these workers are low and they rely on tips. So if you're feeling flush, share the wealth.

- **Bars:** A dollar per drink is standard, although giving more might get you faster service for the next round.

- **Hotels:** Room service expects 10 to 15 percent. Give bellboys a few dollars per bag. It's up to you if you want to leave a tip for housekeeping, and the amount depends on the hotel and the length of your stay; leave cash on the dresser when you check out.

- **Manicures, haircuts, and other beauty treatments:** The usual is 10 to 20 percent. A good tip can also help get you squeezed in for a last-minute appointment when you need one.

- It's customary to tip **service staff such as house cleaners, doormen, and superintendents** around the holidays. The amount is entirely up to you, but a generous tip will help shoot you to the top of the list when you need help installing an air conditioner or new blinds.

How to Select a Bottle of Wine

If you're interested in wine and want to learn more about it, consider taking an in-depth seminar. If you just need to buy the occasional bottle, here's help.

1. Develop a rapport with a good local wine store and make it your first stop for a recommendation. Tell the employee who or what you're buying for, what you'll be eating, and—most important—your budget.

2. Over time you'll become familiar with wines that *you* like, but buying wine for someone else can be tricky. Getting a recommendation from your buddy at the wine store is the safest bet.

3. No one who really knows wine will say that you can't get a good bottle of wine for $15. *Expensive* does not automatically translate to *better*.

4. When you're at a restaurant, ask the server or sommelier (a wine steward or the person in charge of a restaurant's wine list) for a recommendation. It's helpful to know one type of red and one type of white wine that you like so that

you can give the sommelier something to go on. They'll suggest either a red or white depending on your choices for courses. Red wines are generally better for heavy dishes involving meats and pasta; white wines usually pair better with chicken, fish, and salads.

5. Reading a wine's label can offer some clues to the style and potential characteristics of the wine. For example, the alcohol by volume (ABV) is a good indicator of intensity; wines that are 14 percent ABV or more are usually full-bodied, and those that are 12 percent or less ABV are lighter. Wines from warmer regions are often fruitier, whereas wines from cooler regions tend to be sweeter. A wine shop employee or sommelier can explain other details on the label to help you recognize characteristics the next time you're ordering.

6. Consider ordering wine by the glass if the restaurant offers this option. This is a great way to explore new styles without having to commit to the quantity (or price) of a full bottle.

Cooking Tips

Everyone, regardless of gender, should know how to prepare at least one signature dish. If you're a bit uncertain of your skills in the kitchen, keep these simple tips in mind.

- Start with basic recipes that use just three or four ingredients, until you gain more experience.

- When following a recipe, read it through before starting to make sure you have everything you need and understand all the directions.

- Buy the best-quality food available. It will taste better and is better for you.

- Chicken should always be cooked completely; pork should be cooked well, but not too well or it will quickly dry out. Beef can be safely served very rare (as long as it's fresh and from a trustworthy source); how it's cooked depends on personal preference.

- Cutting into a piece of meat to see if it's done will allow the juices to escape and dry it out. Instead, use a meat thermometer to determine when it's done to your liking.

- Don't adjust the flame once you set meat in a pan—doing so will dry it out. Better to start cooking it over a lower flame and cook it longer. The more you cook, the better your judgment will be about when meats are done.

- Spices make an enormous difference in a recipe. Branch out from salt and pepper and experiment with a variety of seasonings. When using herbs, fresh is best; you can always freeze them and take out what you need before you cook. Herbs need about three minutes to defrost.

- To get the most flavor and nutrients out of vegetables, steam them instead of boiling.

"A good cook is like a sorceress who dispenses happiness."

—Elsa Schiaparelli, Italian fashion designer

One Great Recipe

At some point, you will likely experience the feeling of panic that accompanies the unexpected arrival of guests right around dinnertime. You look in your cabinets only to find canned soup and crackers that expired two months ago. You don't want to be the hostess who orders Chinese takeout, yet you're scrambling for something to make. Keep this simple yet delicious recipe on hand for those times when you need to throw together an impressive dish in no time.

Tomato Mozzarella Pasta
Serves 4

Ingredients

1 large can (28 oz.) whole, peeled tomatoes

2–3 garlic cloves, minced

1 tablespoon dried oregano

1 tablespoon dried parsley

Chopped fresh basil (to taste)

Red pepper flakes (to taste)

Olive oil

1 box (1 lb.) dried fusilli pasta

1 pound fresh buffalo mozzarella

1 jar tomato sauce

Directions

Bring a large pot of water to a boil. Cut tomatoes and place in a medium-sized pot. Add garlic, oregano, parsley, and basil. Cook on low/medium heat. While this is cooking, soak red pepper flakes in just enough olive oil to lightly coat the pasta when it's finished cooking. Add pasta to boiling water and cook according to directions on the box. While the pasta is cooking, cut the mozzarella into small pieces, about ½-inch squares. You may not use all the cheese. When the pasta is done cooking, drain in a colander and then return pasta to the large pot. Add pepper flakes with olive oil, and mix. Then add the tomato sauce and the tomato-garlic mixture and mix. Add the mozzarella last and mix well.

MIND,
BODY,
AND
SPIRIT

Self-Defense Techniques

Defending yourself is instinctive. You may not be able to remember a five-part combat move when a 200-pound guy is choking you, but you sure know how to bite, scratch, and slap. The following techniques can help you use those instincts to protect yourself. And if you need help, yell "fire" instead of "help" or "rape." People are more likely to respond immediately to the former than the latter (sad but true).

• Get in the habit of always being alert and aware of your surroundings. If you know what's going on around you, you're more likely to be prepared for anything. Trust your gut, use common sense, and make the following behaviors part of your routine.

  a. If you find yourself in unsafe surroundings, look around and assess the situation—who's there, where the dark corners are, how to escape quickly, and so on.

  b. When entering an alley, parking lot, or building, quickly check to see if anyone is behind you.

c. Don't wear earphones when walking alone. You need to be aware of potential threats.

• If someone grabs you from behind, try to bash his face with the back of your head. The ear is a vulnerable area; reach your arm back and either slap it (knuckles will hurt more than the palm) or grab it and pull as hard as you can.

• The nose is also a weak and vulnerable area. Open your hand and strike it with the meaty base of your palm in an upward direction (figure A).

Figure A

You can cause a severe nosebleed or even break the nose if the blow is strong enough.

- If your attacker is facing you and holding you by the shoulders or choking you, throw your arms up between his as if you were pushing back your hair. Break his grip by bringing your arms down outside of his and pushing his arms down at the elbows (figure B).

Figure B

- If someone is on top of you, he'll try to subdue you—expect a punch and you won't be as dazed by it. Hold his head on both sides and rake your thumbs across his eyes. Pull an ear as hard as you can toward your chest, hold onto his arms to pull yourself up, and bite his neck or face. When he tries to pull away, bite again. Bring your knee into his groin, then run.

- The groin is one of the most painful places to target. Cup your hand, keep your arm loose, and slap (figure C). This will hurt more than a targeted punch. Bring your knee into his groin if he's holding you close, or kick.

Figure C

How to Perform a Breast Self-Examination

You should examine your breasts once a month by how they look and feel. Always check them around the same time each month because breasts change before and during your menstrual cycle. A good time is a week after your period starts. A BSE takes ten minutes and can be a lifesaver—literally. According to the National Breast Cancer Foundation, 40 percent of diagnosed breast cancers are detected by women who have felt a lump.

1. Sit or stand in front of a mirror, relax your arms at your sides, and take a good look at the girls. You're looking for changes in the appearance of the nipples, redness, irritation, dimples in the skin, or discolorations. Look at them from both the front and the side and in the following positions: with your arms down, with your hands on your hips, with your arms above your head, and with your palms pressed together in front of your forehead. Then check them out while leaning forward, with your hands on your knees. After practicing this routine for a few months, you'll notice right away if anything is amiss.

2. Raise one arm, put it behind your head, and use your opposite hand to examine your breast. Here's what you're looking for: anything that feels odd or wasn't there before (which is why you should get in the habit of doing this every month). Lumps and bumps in breasts are normal, but if you notice changes or find a lump in one breast that isn't mirrored in the other (especially in the top outer part of the breast), see a doctor.

3. With the pads of your index, middle, and ring fingers, start at the top of your armpit and move your fingers down until they are below your breast. Now go back up, moving your fingers a bit toward the center of your body. Go from your collarbone to beneath your breasts and from armpits to breastbone. Try not to take your hand off your breast during the exam so that you don't miss a spot.

4. Pass your fingertips over each area three times with light, medium, and firm pressure. This will let you feel all the layers of breast tissue.

5. After feeling your entire breast, gently squeeze the nipple to make sure there is no discharge.

If you feel like something isn't right, see a doctor immediately. Breast cancer is less dangerous when detected early.

Check Your Chest

According to the National Breast Cancer Foundation, one in eight women in the United States will be diagnosed with breast cancer. But don't lose hope. If the disease is detected early in the localized stage via methods such as monthly self-exams (as well as mammograms and annual clinical exams), the five-year survival rate is 100 percent.

How to Perform the Heimlich Maneuver

Hopefully you'll never need to perform this lifesaving technique, but it's essential to know how.

1. Get the choking person to stand. Calmly state that you know the Heimlich maneuver and can help.

2. Stand behind the person with your legs apart (in order to support him if he loses consciousness). Wrap your arms around his waist.

3. Make a fist with your dominant hand and place it, with your thumb tucked in, against his stomach, just above the belly button.

4. Hold your fist with the other hand. Push your fist into the abdomen five times with a quick "inward and up" motion. This will force the diaphragm to move air out of the lungs, creating an artificial cough. Each thrust should be forceful, as if you were trying to jerk him off his feet.

5. Repeat as necessary. Sometimes, it will take several thrusts to dislodge the obstruction.

*Push your fist into the abdomen with
an "inward and up" motion.*

Health Tips for Women

Taking good care of yourself is probably the most important thing a woman can do. So don't delay!

Exams

- **Physical:** Once a year

- **Blood pressure:** At least every two years, or more often if you have a family history of hypertension

- **Cholesterol levels:** Every five years

- **Skin:** Once a year (watch on your own for changes in moles)

- **Dental checkups:** Every six months

- **Gynecological checkups:** Once a year, with Pap smears every two to three years

- **Mammograms:** Yearly with your gynecological checkups beginning at age 40

- **Self-breast exams:** Every month, starting in your teens

Diet and Exercise

- Drink lots of water (eight glasses per day is recommended).

- Eat healthful foods. An easy rule of thumb: look for foods as close to their natural state as possible. (No, there is no natural state of an Oreo.)

- Not only will diets high in saturated and trans fats add weight fast, they will also increase cholesterol levels and your risk for heart disease, which is the number one killer of both men and women. Checking your blood pressure and cholesterol, exercising, and maintaining a balanced diet will help reduce your risk for heart disease.

- Because you lose iron every month during menses, make sure you get enough of it in your diet. Meat, fish, poultry, peas, beans, potatoes, and leafy vegetables are all good sources of iron. Other important nutrients to be aware of: protein, folic acid, omega-3 fatty acids, calcium, magnesium, vitamin D, antioxidants, and vitamin C.

- Be active, preferably every day. Even if it's just a 20-minute walk around your neighborhood, it's better than nothing.

Vitamins

A well-balanced diet should give you all the nutrients you need, but maintaining that well-balanced diet every day can be tricky. If you take vitamins, choose wisely; just because it's a vitamin doesn't make it good for you. There are no rules dictating that what's listed on the label is what's in the capsules. Some vitamins have been found to contain mercury, arsenic, and lead. Those made from organic whole foods are your best bet. They won't be cheap, but they also won't contain synthetic products that your body can't digest.

> NOTE: If you take regular medication, adding vitamins could be a bad combination. Talk to your doctor first.

How to Nurture a Sense of Humor

All the world loves a clown, as the saying goes. You don't have to be the next great comedic talent, but a person who knows how to laugh (at herself especially) is always fun to have around. On top of enjoying your life a lot more, you'll also be invited to more parties! Everyone likes the girl who can roll with the punches. You will, too.

- Be grateful for the good stuff. It's easy to get hung up on things that are minor compared to all the positives, such as a wonderful family, supportive friends, and a fulfilling job.

- Don't expect to change overnight. This isn't about developing a fondness for knock-knock jokes; it's an entire attitude about life. Learn to laugh at your mistakes instead of beating yourself up over them. Accept that bad things happen and that you're wasting time by being angry or bitter.

- Think about all the times you've worried about something over which you had no control. How useful was that? You'll notice that by changing your outlook, challenges become less intimidating and you'll be able to confront an obstacle that would have derailed you before.

- Look for the humor all around you. You can choose to focus on either the negative in the world or the positive. Choose the positive and your whole outlook on life will change drastically.

- Try not to take things so seriously. Loosen up.

- The same goes for criticism from those who mean it caringly and constructively. Nobody's perfect, and we could all use a little help. Take it when offered.

- People respond to the way you approach them, and if you try your hardest to go through life with an upbeat attitude you'll have it reflected back at you. Sincerely positive people make big impressions.

Tips for Good Posture

As your mother used to say, stand up straight! Slouching gives the impression of being weak and defensive. Paying attention to your body and constantly reminding yourself to straighten up will pay off: Not only will you feel better, you'll come across as more confident and in control.

- When standing or walking, pull your shoulders back and down, look straight ahead (not down), with your chin parallel to the ground. Your toes should point forward.

- Once a day, stand in front of a mirror, relax your shoulders, and make sure they're level. If you regularly carry a purse on the same shoulder, you may find that you automatically hike up that shoulder, even without a purse on it.

- If you've been slouching for years, it will take real effort to keep your back, shoulders, and neck aligned. Stretching and strengthening exercises will help you sit up straight, and you'll start becoming more aware of hunching over. Try yoga or Pilates classes to build up your core muscles.

- If you sit at a desk or in front of a computer for long periods, you may be tempted to let your body get lazy and do whatever it wants. It's best to sit with both feet on the floor, or use a footrest if you can't reach the floor while maintaining a straight back.

- A firm but not rigid mattress supports your spine all through the night, effectively giving you better posture while you sleep.

- Standing and sitting up straight are good for you—really! People who regularly have a rounded back and slumped shoulders tend to become sick more often than those with good posture. This has to do with your chest being concave and allowing sickness to settle there. It sounds New Age-y, but it's one more reason to sit up straight.

How to De-Stress

Stress is one of the biggest contributors to disease. Although this feeling can be a powerful motivator, you should have a way to shake off too much tension before it snowballs into something more serious.

- How you respond to and handle stress is an indication of what you need to do to remedy it. If not much fazes you, you might just need to sit down with a book and a cup of tea, watch TV, or do anything else that will let your brain turn to mush for a while.

- On the other hand, if you tend to internalize stress, become increasingly tense, lose sleep, and snap at people for no reason, you'll need to be a little more proactive. The first step is to learn to identify when you are entering that mode, so your stress-induced misery doesn't blindside you and prevent you from doing something about it.

- Exercise is a major ally in battling stress. You might not be able to punch that incompetent moron from Marketing in the face, but you can direct all that energy to a punching bag or an exhausting run. Making your body work hard will help relieve some of the pressure that's plaguing you.

- Many people say they are happier and less stressed when they eat healthful foods. Fruits, veggies, and whole grains naturally give you more energy, whereas junk food can actually raise your stress levels.

- The fascinating thing about stress is that we do it to ourselves. Tough as it is, you can choose whether or not to let something get to you. Since that won't happen overnight, find activities that are soothing, distracting, and happiness-inducing. Long walks, deep breathing, talking to a friend, gardening, crossword puzzles, yoga, painting, taking a bath, sitting on a park bench and soaking up the sun, volunteering, going for a drive and blasting music—anything that lets you focus on something else for a bit.

- Get enough sleep, find a few hours a week for exercise, and devote twenty minutes a day to something relaxing. Taking care of yourself is the ultimate gift you can give yourself, and you'll be a happier, healthier person for it.

Stuff You Should Know That I Can't Tell You

- What you want out of life
- The story of how your parents met
- When to walk away
- Your "nonnegotiables"
- Your signature cocktail
- What makes you happy
- Your family's medical history
- The phone number for a great hair stylist, tailor, and bikini waxer
- When to ask your mom for advice
- How to say "no"
- When to admit you're wrong
- One great joke
- The lyrics to your favorite song
- When to trust your instinct
- How to freshen up in the bathroom in one minute
- How to love yourself exactly as you are

Acknowledgments

Thanks to Sarah O'Brien and the fantastic bunch at Quirk for taking a chance on an unknown kid. Many, many thanks to Blaise and his boundless patience, Dad and Amy, Opa, Oren, Sophie, and Mom. To everyone who contributed words of wisdom: a great big thank-you.